I0166152

Anonymous

The Colorado Election Law

1883

Anonymous

The Colorado Election Law
1883

ISBN/EAN: 9783744666183

Printed in Europe, USA, Canada, Australia, Japan

Cover: Foto ©ninafisch / pixelio.de

More available books at **www.hansebooks.com**

THE COLORADO

ELECTION LAW

~~~~~~~~~

1883.

PUBLISHED BY AUTHORITY.

TIMES STEAM PRINTING HOUSE AND BLANK BOOK MANUFACTORY.

DENVER, COLORADO.

1884.

ELECTION LAW.

Chapter XXXIV., G. S.

SECTION 1. Every male person over the age of twenty-one years, possessing the following qualifications, shall be entitled to vote at all elections:

First—He shall be a citizen of the United States, or, not being a citizen of the United States, he shall have declared his intention according to law to become such citizen not less than four months before he offers to vote.

Second—He shall have resided in this State six months immediately preceding the election at which he offers to vote; in the county, ninety days; and in the ward or precinct, ten days; *Provided*, That no person shall be denied the right to vote at any school district election, nor to hold any school district office, on account of sex. That all acts or parts of acts inconsistent with this act be and the same are hereby repealed.

SEC. 2. No person under guardianship, *non compos mentis*, or insane, shall be qualified to vote at any election, nor shall any person while confined in any public prison be entitled to vote, but every such person who was a qualified elector prior to such imprisonment, and who is released therefrom by pardon or by having served out his full term of imprisonment, shall be vested with all the rights of citizenship except as provided in the constitution.

SEC. 3. For the purposes of voting and eligibility to office, no person shall be deemed to have gained a residence by reason of his presence, or lost it by reason of his absence, while in the civil or military service of the State or of the United States, nor while a student at any institution of learning, nor while kept at public expense in any poorhouse or other asylum, nor while confined in public prison.

SEC. 4. Every qualified elector shall be eligible to hold any office of this State for which he is an elector, except as otherwise provided by the constitution.

SEC. 5. A general election shall be held in the several wards and precincts in this State on the first Tuesday of October, A. D. 1877, 1878 and 1879, and on the Tuesday succeeding the first Monday in November, A. D. 1880, and on the Tuesday succeeding the first Monday of November in every year thereafter.

SEC. 6. At the general election, A. D. 1877, and every alternate year thereafter, there shall be elected in every county of the State the following county officers, to-wit: One county clerk, who shall be *ex officio* recorder of deeds and clerk of the board of county commissioners; one sheriff, one coroner, one treasurer, who shall be collector of taxes; one county superintendent of schools, one county surveyor and one county assessor. There shall also be elected in every county of the State, at the general election, A. D. 1877, and every third year thereafter, one county judge.

SEC. 7. At the general election, A. D. 1878, and every alternate year thereafter, there shall be elected the following State officers, to wit: One governor, one lieutenant-governor, one secretary of State, one State treasurer, one auditor of State, one superintendent of public instruction, and two regents of the university; and in each representative district of the State, such members of the house of representatives as they may severally be entitled to. State senators shall be elected in every senatorial district at the general election in the year when the term of office of senator shall expire in such district respectively; also, on the first Tuesday succeeding the first Monday of November, A. D. 1878, and every alternate year thereafter, there shall be elected the number of representatives in congress to which the State may be entitled.

SEC. 8. At the general election, A. D. 1879, and every third year thereafter, there shall be elected one judge of the supreme court, and in each judicial district of the State one district attorney. At the general election, A. D. 1880, and every fourth year thereafter, there shall be elected such a number of electors of president and vice-president of the United States as the State may be entitled to in the electoral college, and at the general election in 1882, and every sixth year thereafter, there shall be elected in each judicial district one judge of the district court.

SEC. 9. At the general election, A. D. 1877, and annually thereafter, there shall be elected in each county of the State one county commissioner, whose term of office shall be three years, and in each justice's precinct, except wards in incorporated cities, there shall be elected at the general election, A. D. 1877, and annually thereafter, one justice' of the peace and one constable, whose terms of office shall be two years ; and all other officers not herein specified that now are or hereafter may be created shall, unless otherwise provided, be elected on the day of the general election.

SEC. 10. All vacancies in any State or county office, and in the supreme or district courts, unless otherwise provided for by law, shall be filled by appointment by the governor until the next general election after such vacancy occurs, when such vacancy shall be filled by election, and the district judge shall fill all vacancies in the office of district attorney in his district by appointment until the next general election.

SEC. 11. The regular term of office of all State, district, county and precinct officers and of the judges of the supreme court shall commence on the second Tuesday of January next after their election, except as otherwise provided by law.

SEC. 12. The regular term of office of members of the general assembly shall commence on the first Wednesday of December next after their election.

SEC. 13. Any of the said officers that may be elected or appointed to fill vacancies may qualify and enter upon the duties of their office immediately thereafter, and if elected they may hold the same during the unexpired term for which they were elected, and until their successors are elected and qualified, but if appointed they shall hold the same only until their successors are elected and qualified.

SEC. 14. Whenever a vacancy shall occur in the office of senator or member of the house of representatives in any county or counties or district in this State, entitled by law to such senator or representative, the governor shall, upon satisfactory information thereof, and as soon as the necessity is apparent, issue a writ or writs of election to the sheriff or sheriffs of said county or counties, entitled by law to such senator or representative, as aforesaid, directing him to give notice of a special election within such county or counties on a day specified in such writ or writs, for the purpose of filling such vacancy; and the sheriff shall proceed to give notice of the time and place of holding such election, as in other cases, and such election shall be held and conducted, and the returns thereof be made to the county clerks in the same manner and within the time specified in this act.

Sec. 15. Special elections shall be conducted and the results thereof canvassed and certified in all respects as near as practicable in like manner as general elections, except as otherwise provided; but special elections shall not be held, unless when required by public good, and in no case within ninety days next preceding a general election.

Sec. 16. All vacancies in any county or precinct office of any of the several counties of the State, except that of the county commissioner, shall be filled by appointment by the county commissioners of the county in which the vacancy occurs until the next general election, when such vacancy shall be filled by election subject to the provisions of section twenty-nine, article six, of the constitution.

Sec. 17. Whenever the governor appoints a county commissioner to fill a vacancy in any county he shall appoint a person who is a resident of the county and of the commissioner district of the county in which the vacancy exists.

Sec. 18. Whenever any vacancy shall happen in the office of representative in congress from this State, it shall be the duty of the governor to appoint a day to hold a special election to fill such vacancy, and cause notice of such election to be given as required in section twenty of this act.

Sec. 19. The secretary of State shall, at least thirty days previous to any general election, at which officers of the executive department, regents of the university, members of the general assembly, judges of the supreme and district courts, district attorneys, representatives in congress, and presidential electors, are to be elected for a full term, make out and cause to be delivered, or transmitted by registered letter, to the county clerk of each county, a notice in writing, stating that at the next general election the beforementioned officers are to be elected, or so many of such officers as are then to be chosen; when members of the general assembly are to be elected, and are included in such notice, it shall specify the number of the district, and the name of the member or members whose terms of office will expire.

SEC. 20. Whenever there is a vacancy in any of the offices mentioned in the preceding section, which is by law to be filled at the general election, at which county officers are elected, the secretary of State shall, at least thirty days previous to said election, give notice in writing, as provided for in the preceding section, and said notice shall specify the office in which a vacancy exists, the cause of such vacancy, the name of the officer in whose office it has occurred, and the time when his term of office will expire.

SEC. 21. The county clerk shall give notice in writing of each general or special election, in which shall be stated the time when it will be held, and the officers then to be elected, by causing the same to be published in a newspaper having general circulation in the county, and sending a copy of such notice by mail to the judges of election in each precinct, to be posted at the place of voting at least fifteen days before such time.

SEC. 22. County commissioners of the several counties in this State are hereby required to divide their respective counties into as many election precincts for all general and special elections as they may deem expedient for the convenience of voters of said county, and shall designate the house or place in each precinct or ward at which elections are to be holden, and the precincts and places of holding elections thus established shall so remain until changed by the board of commissioners; *Provided*, that the board of county commissioners shall establish at least one election precinct for every five hundred registered voters, as shown by the registry list of the respective counties at the last general election, and shall every year, if necessary, increase the number of election precincts as the number of registered voters shall be increased on said registry list, so that at least one election precinct for every three hundred registered voters may be constituted ; *And provided*, That it shall be the duty of the county commissioners at any time to change any place of holding elections upon a petition of a majority of the voters residing within said precinct ; *And provided further*, That the precincts and wards established and the places designated in which to hold elections at the time of the taking effect of this act shall so remain until changed; *And provided further*, That no new precincts shall be established or polling places changed at a later date than thirty days previous to any election.

SEC. 23. The said boards of county commissioners respectively, at the July session of such board, shall appoint three capable and discreet persons, representing at least two political parties, if practicable, possessing the qualification of electors, to act as judges of the election in each election precinct, at all general and special elections, until their successors are appointed; and the clerk of said board shall make out and deliver, by mail or other safe conveyance, without expense to the county, to each one of the judges so appointed, a notice in writing of their appointment.

SEC. 24. The county commissioners of each county shall provide a ballot box at the expense of the county for each place of voting, which box shall be made of glass, to be kept by the county clerk and recorder of each county and by them delivered over to their successors in office. Each of said ballot boxes shall be circular in form, with a small opening in the top thereof, and enclosed in a square wooden frame with a lid to be fastened by three locks, no two of which can be opened by the same key : one of said keys shall be kept by each of the judges of the election last appointed, to be by them delivered to their successors in office. Should either of said judges die or remove from their precinct, meantime, the key held by him shall be surrendered to the county clerk and recorder, to be by him kept and delivered to the successor of such judge of election. The said ballot boxes shall be by the clerk and recorder of the respective counties delivered to the judges of election within three days immediately preceding any general or special election, to be by him used and returned as hereinafter provided.

SEC. 25. The said judges of election shall choose two persons having similar qualifications with themselves to act as clerks of the election; and the said clerks of election may continue to act as such during the pleasure of the judges of the election.

SEC. 26. If any person appointed to act as a judge of the election as aforesaid shall neglect or refuse to be sworn or affirmed, or to act in such capacity, the place of such person shall be filled by the votes of such qualified voters residing within the precinct as may then be present at the place of election, and the person or persons so elected to fill such vacancy or vacancies shall be and are hereby vested with the same power as if appointed by the board of county commissioners.

SEC. 27. Previous to any votes being taken the judges and clerks of the election shall severally take an oath or affirmation in the following form, to-wit. " I, A. B., do solemnly swear (or affirm) that I will perform the duties of judge (or clerk, as the case may be) according to law, and the best of my ability; that I will studiously endeavor to prevent fraud, deceit and abuse in conducting the same, and that I will not try to ascertain, nor will I disclose, how any elector voted, if, in the discharge of my duties as judge (or clerk, as the case may be) knowledge shall come to me as to how any elector shall have voted, unless called upon to disclose the same before some court of justice.

SEC. 28. In case there shall be no judge, justice of the peace, or other person qualified by law to administer an oath, present at the opening of the election, to administer the oath mentioned in the preceding section, it shall be lawful for the judges of the election, and they are hereby empowered to administer the oaths or affirmations to each other, and to the clerks of the election, and the person administering such oaths or affirmations shall cause an entry thereof to be made and subscribed by him, and prefixed to the poll books.

Sec. 29. Whenever it shall become impossible or inconvenient to hold an election at the place designated therefor the judges of election, after having assembled at or as near as practicable to such place, and before receiving any vote, may adjourn to the nearest convenient place for holding the election and at such adjourned place forthwith proceed with the election.

Sec. 30. Upon adjourning any election, as provided in the preceding section, the judges shall cause proclamation thereof to be made, and shall station a constable or some other proper person at the place where the adjournment was made from to notify all elector [electors] arriving at such place of adjournment and the place to which it was made.

Sec. 31. At all elections held under this act, the polls shall be opened at seven o'clock in the morning, and continue open until seven o'clock in the evening of the same day; *Provided, however*, That if a full board of judges shall not attend at the hour of seven o'clock in the morning, and it shall be necessary for the electors present to appoint judges to conduct the election as hereinbefore prescribed, the election may, in that event, commence at any hour before the time for closing the polls shall arrive, as the case may require. Upon the opening of the polls, proclamation shall be made by one of the clerks, and thirty minutes before the closing of the polls proclamation shall be made in like manner that the polls will close in thirty minutes.

Sec. 32. Every elector shall vote by ballot, which shall be numbered in the order in which it shall be received, and the number recorded by the election officers on the list of voters opposite the name of the voter who presents the ballot. Each person offering to vote shall deliver his ballot to one of the judges in the presence of the board. The ballot shall be a paper ticket, which shall contain, written or printed, or partly written and partly printed, the names of the persons for whom the elector intends to vote, and shall designate the office to which each person so named by him is intended to be voted for.

SEC. 33. The names of all persons voted for by any elector, at any general or special election, shall be on one ballot.

SEC. 34. If any elector shall vote more than once, or having voted once, shall offer to vote again at any election, or shall offer to deposit in the ballot box at any election more than one ballot, he shall be deemed guilty of a misdemeanor, and on conviction thereof shall be fined not exceeding one hundred dollars or imprisoned in the county jail not exceeding sixty days.

SEC. 35. Each elector shall in full view deliver to one of the judges of election a single ballot.

SEC. 36. The judge to whom any ticket may be delivered, shall, upon the receipt thereof, pronounce in an audible voice the name of the elector, and if no objection shall be made to him, and the judges are satisfied that he is a legal elector and is duly registered, the ballot shall be numbered and immediately be put in the ballot box without inspecting the names written or printed thereon, and the clerks of the election shall enter the name of the elector and number in the poll books.

SEC. 37. The judges of election, in determining the residence of a person offering to vote, shall be governed by the following rules, so far as they may be applicable:

First—That place shall be considered and held to be the residence of a person in which his habitation is fixed, and to which, whenever he is absent, he has the intention of returning.

Second—A person shall not be considered or held to have lost his residence, who shall leave his home and go into another State, territory or county of this State, for temporary purposes merely, with an intention of returning.

Third—A person shall not be considered or held to have gained a residence in this State, or in any county in this State, when retaining his home or domicile elsewhere.

Fourth—If a person remove to any other State, or to any of the territories, with the intention of making it his permanent residence, he shall be considered and held to have lost his residence in this State.

Fifth—If a person remove from one county, precinct or ward in this State to any other county, precinct or ward in this State, with the intention of making it his permanent residence, he shall be considered and held to have lost his residence in the county, precinct or ward from which he removed.

SEC. 38.   If a person offering to vote be challenged as unqualified, by one of the judges of election, or by any elector, one of the judges shall tender to him the following oath or affirmation: " You do solemnly swear (or affirm) that you will fully and truly answer all such questions as shall be put to you touching your place of residence and qualification of an elector at this election."

First—If the person be challenged as unqualified, on the ground that he is not a citizen, and will not exhibit his papers pertaining to his naturalization, the judges, or one of them, shall put the following questions : *First*—Are you a citizen of the United States ?   *Second*—Are you a native or naturalized citizen ; and, if neither, have you declared your intention to become a citizen, conformably to the laws of the United States, on the subject of naturalization, at least four months previous to to-day ?   *Third*—Have you become a citizen of the United States by reason of the naturalization of your parents, or one of them ?   *Fourth*—Where were your parents, or one of them, naturalized ? If the person offering to vote claims to be a naturalized citizen of the United States, or that he has four months previous to the election declared his intention to become such, he shall state, under oath, where and in what courts he was naturalized.

Second—If the person be challenged as unqualified, on the ground that he has not resided in this State for six months immediately preceding the election, the judges, or one of them, shall put the following questions : *First*—Have you resided in this State for six months immediately preceding this election, and during that time have you retained a home or domicile elsewhere ?   *Second*—Have you been absent from this State within the six months immediately preceding this election ?   *Third*—If so, when you left, was it for a temporary purpose, with the design of returning, or did you intend remaining away ?   *Fourth*—

Did you, while absent, look upon and regard this State as your home? *Fifth*—Did you, while absent, vote in any State or territory?

Third—If the person be challenged on the ground that he has not resided in the county thirty [90] days or in the precinct or ward ten days, one of the judges shall question him as to his residence in the county, precinct or ward in a manner similar to the before-mentioned method of questioning a person as to his residence in this State.

Fourth—If the person be challenged as unqualified on the ground that he is not twenty-one years of age, the judges, or one of them, shall put the following question: Are you twenty-one years of age, to the best of your knowledge and belief? The judges of the election, or one of them, shall put all such other questions to the person challenged under the respective heads aforesaid as may be necessary to test his qualifications as an elector at that election.

SEC. 39. If the person challenged as aforesaid shall refuse to answer fully any question which shall be put to him as aforesaid, the judges shall reject his vote.

SEC. 40. If the challenge be not withdrawn after the person offering to vote shall have answered the questions put to him as aforesaid, one of the judges shall tender to him the following oath: " You do solemnly swear (or affirm) that you are a citizen of the United States (or declared your intention of becoming such at least four months previous to this election), of the age of twenty-one years; that you have been a resident of this State for six months next preceding this election, and have not retained a home or domicile elsewhere; that you have been for the last thirty [90] days, and now are, a resident of this county; that you have been for the last ten days, and now are, a resident of this precinct (or ward, as the case may be), and that you have not voted at this election."

SEC. 41. If any person shall refuse to take the oath or affirmation so tendered his vote shall be rejected: *Provided*, That after such oath shall have been taken the judges may nevertheless refuse to permit such person to vote if they shall be satisfied that he is not a legal voter.

SEC. 42. Whenever any person's vote shall be received, after having taken the oath or affirmation prescribed in section forty (40) of this act, it shall be the duty of the clerks of the election to write on the poll books at the end of the person's name, " sworn."

SEC. 43. It shall be the duty of any judge of election to challenge any person offering to vote whom he shall believe not to be qualified as an elector.

SEC. 44. It shall be the duty of the judges of election, immediately before proclamation is made of the opening of the polls, to open the ballot box in the presence of the people there assembled and turn it upside down so as to empty it of everything that may be in it, and then lock it securely; and it shall not be reopened until for the purpose of counting the ballots therein at the close of the election.

SEC. 45. For the preservation of order as well as the securing of the judges and clerks of the election from insult and abuse it shall be the duty of any constable or constables residing within the precinct, who shall be designated for the purpose by the judges of the election to attend to all elections within his precinct, and the judges of election are hereby authorized and empowered to appoint one or more special constables to assist in preserving order during the elections and until the votes are canvassed.

SEC. 46. Constables or special constables appointed or requested by the judges of election to preserve peace at the polls, shall each receive two dollars and a half per day for their services, payable out of the county treasury.

SEC. 47. Each clerk of the election shall keep a poll list which shall contain one column headed, " Names of voters," and one column headed, " Number on ballot." The name and the number on the ballot of each elector voting shall be entered by each clerk in regular succession under the said headings in his poll list.

SEC. 48. The polls at any election shall not be closed, after once being opened, until they are finally closed in the evening.

SEC. 49. As soon as the polls at any election shall have finally closed, the judges shall immediately open

the ballot-box and proceed to count the votes polled, and
the counting thereof shall be commenced and continued
until finished before the judges and clerks shall adjourn.
They shall first count the number of ballots in the box.
If the ballots shall be found to exceed the number of
names entered on each of the poll lists, the numbers upon
the ballots shall be examined without opening the ballots,
and if it be found that those in excess of the total number
on the poll list be not numbered, they shall be destroyed.
If it be found that there is more than one ballot having the
same number, the ballots having the same numbers shall
be replaced in the box and shaken up, and one of the
judges shall publicly draw out and destroy all but one of
said ballots. When the ballots and the poll lists agree, or
as above provided, have been made to agree, the board shall
proceed to count the votes; each ballot shall be read and
counted separately, and every name on each ballot shall be
read and marked upon the tally lists before another ballot
is proceeded with, and the entire number of ballots shall be
read and counted and placed upon the tally lists in like
manner, and when all of the ballots have been counted as
herein provided the board shall estimate and publish the
votes. The judges of election shall permit each candidate
or their friends, not exceeding two in number, upon the
written request of such candidate, to be present while the
ballots are being received and counted.

SEC. 50. As the judges of election shall open and
read the tickets, each clerk shall, upon tally lists prepared
for the purpose, carefully mark down the votes each candidate shall have received in separate lines, with the name
of such candidate at the end of the line, and the office
it is designed by the voters such candidate shall fill; but
if on such canvassing two or more tickets shall be found
deccitfully folded together such tickets shall be rejected.

SEC. 51. As soon as all the votes shall have been
read off and counted, the judges of election shall make out
a certificate under their hands, and attested by the clerks,
stating the number of votes each candidate received, designating the office for which such person received such vote
or votes, and the number he did receive, the number being
expressed in words at full length, and in numerical figures,
such entry to be made, as nearly as circumstances will

admit, in the following form, to-wit: At an election held at the house of ———, in ——— precinct or ward, in the county of ——— and State of Colorado, on the ——— day of ——— in the year of our Lord one thousand eight hundred and ———, the following-named persons received the number of votes annexed to their respective names for the following described offices, to wit: Whole number of votes cast were ———. A. B. had seventy-two (72) votes for governor; C. D. had seventy-one (71) votes for governor; E. F. had seventy-two (72) votes for lieutenant-governor; G. H. had sixty-nine (69) votes for lieutenant-governor; J. K. had sixty-eight (68) votes for representative in congress; L. M. had seventy (70) votes for representative in congress; N. O. had seventy-two (72) votes for representative; P. Q. had seventy-one (71) votes for representative; R. S. had eighty-four (84) votes for sheriff; T. W. had sixty (60) votes for sheriff; and in the same manner for any other persons voted for.

Certified by us:

A. B. ⎫ Judges
C. D. ⎬ of
E. F. ⎭ Election.

Attest :
G. H. ⎱ Clerks of
I. J. ⎰ Election.

And the said certificate, together with one of the lists of voters, and one of the tally papers, shall then be enclosed and sealed up, under cover, and directed to the clerk of the county in which such election is held, and the packet thus sealed shall be sent by registered letter where practicable, otherwise it shall be conveyed by one of the judges or clerks of the election, to be determined by lot if they cannot agree otherwise, within six days of the closing of the polls. And if any judge or clerk of an election, after having been deputed by the judges of election, at which he served as judge or clerk, to carry the poll book of such election to the clerk of the county, shall fail or neglect to deliver such poll book to the said clerk, within the time prescribed by law, safe, with the seal unbroken, he·shall for every offense forfeit and pay the sum of five hundred dollars, for the use of the county, to be recovered in the name of the commissioners of the county.

by an action of debt in any court of competent jurisdiction; *Provided*, That informality in the delivering of the poll books as directed in this section shall not invalidate the vote of any precinct when said poll books shall have been delivered previous to the canvassing of the votes of such election by the county board of canvassers. When all the votes shall have been read and counted, the ballots, together with one of the tally lists, shall be returned to the ballot box and the opening in the glass part thereof shall be carefully sealed and each of the judges shall place his private mark on said seal, the wooden cover shall then be locked, and each of the judges shall preserve one of the keys thereof as herein provided. This box shall then be delivered by one of the clerks of the election who is of the opposite political party from the judge or clerk chosen to take charge of and deliver the certificate and tally list, which clerk shall at once and with all convenient speed take said box to the office of the county clerk and recorder and safely deliver it to such officer, taking his delivery receipt therefor.

SEC. 52. If any judge or the judges of any election shall wilfully and maliciously refuse to receive the ballot of any qualified elector, who shall take or offer to take the oath prescribed by this act, in such case every judge so refusing or neglecting to receive the vote or ballot, when the same shall be presented, shall be liable to be indicted, and on conviction thereof shall be fined five hundred dollars, and imprisoned not exceeding thirty days; and for every refusal or neglect to receive such vote, the party aggrieved may have an action on the case against the said judge or judges; the damages in such case shall not exceed the sum of five hundred dollars.

SEC. 53. On the tenth day after the close of the election, or sooner, if all the returns be received, the clerk of the county, taking to his assistance two justices of the peace of his county, one at least of whom shall belong to a different political party than himself, if any such there be in the county, shall proceed to open the said returns, and make abstracts of the votes in the following manner: The abstract of votes for electors for president and vice-president of the United States shall be on one sheet, and the abstract of votes for representative in congress shall be

3e

on another sheet, and the abstract of votes for regents of
the university shall be on another sheet, and the [abstract
of] votes for officers of the executive department shall be on
another sheet, and the abstract of votes for senators shall
be on another sheet, and the abstract of votes for representatives shall be on another sheet, and the abstract of votes
for judges of the supreme court shall be on another sheet,
and the abstract of votes for judges of the district court
and district attorneys shall be on another sheet, and the
abstract of votes for county and precinct officers shall be on
another sheet; and it shall be the duty of the said clerk of
the county immediately to make out a certificate of election
to each of the persons having the highest number of votes
for county and precinct officers, respectively, and cause
such certificate to be delivered to the person entitled to it.
If any two or more persons have an equal number of votes
for the same county or precinct office, and a higher number
than any other person, the county clerk and his assistants
aforesaid shall immediately determine by lot which of the
two candidates shall be elected.

SEC. 54.   The clerk of the county, immediately after
making out abstracts of votes given in his county, shall
make a copy of such abstract and deliver or transmit the
same in a registered package by mail to the office of the
secretary of State; the original abstracts he shall file and
record in a book in his office to be kept for that purpose.
He shall also certify to the abstracts and copies, and affix
thereto the county seal, and the said clerk shall respectively
endorse on the back of the envelope in which the said certified copies are enclosed, " Certified copy of the abstract of
votes cast for governor, etc., members of the general assembly, etc., (as the case may be) cast at the regular election in
———— county, ————, 18—."

SEC. 55.   Whenever it shall so happen that the county
clerk shall die, be absent, or from any casualty be prevented
from opening the returns of votes at any election, it shall
be lawful for his deputy to discharge the duties required of
such clerk by law; which deputy shall be appointed by the
majority of county commissioners when said clerk has
failed to appoint a deputy.

SEC. 56.   The abstract of votes cast in each county
for the officers of the executive department shall be sealed

up by the county clerks of said counties, and delivered or transmitted in a registered package by mail to the secretary of State, directed to the speaker of the house of representatives. Upon the organization of the house the secretary of State shall deliver to the speaker of the house all of the returns for officers of the executive department that he shall have received, and upon the receipt of the same by the speaker of the house of representatives he shall, before proceeding to other business, open and publish the same in the presence of a majority of the members of both houses of the general assembly, who shall for that purpose assemble in the hall of the house of representatives. The person having the highest number of votes for either of said offices shall be declared duly elected by the presiding officer of the joint assembly, but if two or more have an equal and the highest number of votes for the same office, one of them shall be chosen thereto by the two houses on joint ballot.

SEC. 57. The governor, secretary of State, auditor of State, treasurer of State and attorney-general, or any three of them, shall constitute the board of State canvassers, and shall canvass the abstracts of votes cast in the different counties of the State for electors of president and vice-president, for representative in congress, for regents of the university, for judges of the supreme and district courts, for district attorneys, and for senators and representatives.

SEC. 58. If from any county no such abstract of votes shall have been received within the twenty-five days next after any election, by the secretary of State, he shall dispatch a special messenger to obtain a copy of the same from the county clerk of such county, and such county clerk shall immediately on demand of such messenger make out and deliver to him the copy required, which copy of the abstract of votes the messenger shall deliver to the secretary of State without delay. The said messenger shall receive as compensation for his services three dollars per day, and fifteen cents for each mile traveled in going to and returning from the county seat of said county, by the usual route, to be paid out of the State treasury.

SEC. 59. For the purpose of canvassing the result of elections, the State board of canvassers shall meet at the office of the secretary of State at ten o'clock of the forenoon of the twenty-fifth day after any election for any of the officers mentioned in section fifty three (53) of this act, if it be not on Sunday ; if it be on Sunday, then they shall meet on the twenty-sixth day, when they shall, if the returns from all the counties of the State be in the possession of the secretary of State, proceed to canvass the votes. If the returns are not all in they shall adjourn from time-to time, as they deem proper, to wait the receipt of all returns ; *Provided, however,* That on the last Wednesday of December next after the election, they shall canvass the votes, whether all the returns be received or not ; *And also provided,* That on the year upon which there is elected electors of president and vice-president, the State board of canvassers shall meet at the secretary of State's office on the last secular day of November, in the year of the election, and proceed to canvass the votes cast for said electors.

SEC. 60. The State board of canvassers, when met in accordance with the law, and a quorum (three) being present, shall proceed to examine and make statement of the whole number of votes given at any such election for all of the officers mentioned in section fifty-three (53) of this act that shall have been voted for in said election ; which statements shall show the names of the persons to whom such votes shall have been given for either of said offices, and the whole number given to each, distinguishing the several districts and counties in which they were given ; they shall certify such statements to be correct and subscribe their names thereto, and they shall thereupon determine what persons have been by the greatest number of votes duly elected to such offices, or either of them, and shall endorse and subscribe on such statements a certificate of their determination and deliver them to the secretary of State.

SEC. 61. If any two or more persons have an equal and the highest number of votes for member of either house of the general assembly, for judge of the supreme or district courts, for district attorney, or for regent of the university, or electors of president and vice-president, the State canvassers shall proceed to determine by lot which of the candidates shall be declared elected: Reasonable notice shall be given to such candidates of the time when such election will be so determined.

Sec. 62. The secretary of State shall record in his office in a book to be kept by him for that purpose each certified statement and determination, as made by the board of State canvassers, and shall without delay make out and transmit to each of the persons thereby declared to be elected, a certificate of his election, certified by him under his seal of office ; and he shall also forthwith cause a copy of such certified statement and determination to be published in a newspaper published at the seat of government.

Sec. 63. Upon the day fixed by law for the assembling of the general assembly the secretary of State shall lay before each house a list of the members elected thereto, with the districts they represent, in accordance with the returns in his office.

Sec. 64. The secretary of State shall prepare lists of the names of the electors of president and vice-president of the United States, elected at any election, procure thereto the signature of the governor, affix the seal of the State to the same, and deliver one of such certificates thus signed to each of said electors, on or before the first Wednesday in December next after such election.

Sec. 65. The electors of president and vice-president of the United States shall convene at the capital of the State, on the first Wednesday of December, next after their election, at the hour of twelve o'clock at noon of that day ; and if there shall be any vacancy in the office of electors, occasioned by death, refusal to act, neglect to attend, or other cause, the elector or electors present shall immediately proceed to fill such vacancy in the electoral college ; and when the vacancies shall have been filled as above provided they shall proceed to perform the duties required of such electors by the constitution and laws of the United States, and vote for president and vice-president by open ballot.

Sec. 66. Every elector of this State for the election of president and vice-president of the United States, hereafter elected, who shall attend and give his vote for those officers at the time and place appointed by law, shall be entitled to receive the sum of five dollars per day for each day's attendance at such election, and fifteen cents per mile for each mile he shall travel in going to and returning from the place where the electors shall meet, by the most usual traveled route, to be paid out of the general contingent fund, and the auditor of State shall audit the amount and draw his warrant for the same. There shall be an election held in this State for the election of such electors at the times appointed by any law of congress or the constitution of the United States for such election, and when such election shall be special the same shall be called, held, and the votes polled, canvassed in all respects as at a general election, and the duties of the electors so elected shall be the same as prescribed by law for electors elected at a general election.

SEC. 67. Whenever the judges of election in any precinct or ward discover in the canvassing of votes that the name of any candidate voted for be misspelled, or the initial letters of his Christian name or names be transposed or omitted in part or altogether on the ballot, the vote or votes for such candidates shall be counted for him if the intention of the elector to vote for him be apparent ; and whenever the board of county canvassers or of State canvassers, or the speaker of the house of representatives, when authorized by law to canvass votes or returns, shall find the returns from any precinct, ward, county or district (as the case may be) do not strictly conform to the requirements of law in the making, certifying and returning the same, the votes polled in such precinct, ward, county or district shall, nevertheless, be canvassed and counted, if such returns shall be sufficiently explicit to enable such boards, or any person or persons authorized to canvass votes and returns, to determine therefrom how many votes were polled for the several persons who were candidates and voted for at the election of which the votes are being canvassed.

SEC. 68. If upon proceeding to canvass the votes it shall clearly appear to the canvassers that in any statement produced to them certain matters are omitted in such statement which should have been inserted, or that any mistakes which are clerical merely, exist, they shall cause the said statement to be sent by one of their number (whom they shall depute for that purpose) to the precinct or ward judges, or to the county board of canvassers (as the case may be) from whom they were received, to have the same corrected, and the judges of election or county clerk (as the case may be) when so demanded, shall make such correction as the facts of the case require, but shall not change or alter any decision before made by them, but shall only cause their canvass to be correctly stated; and the canvassing board may adjourn from day to day for the purpose of obtaining and receiving such statement; *Provided always*, That they shall not delay counting past the day provided by law for the completion of the canvass.

SEC. 69. Judges and clerks of election shall each receive as compensation for their services two and a half dollars per day of twelve hours or fractional part thereof of over four hours, and it shall be the duty of the clerk of each county, on the receipt of the election returns of any general or special election, to make out his certificate stating therein the compensation to which the judges and clerks of such election may be entitled for their services and lay the same before the board of county commissioners at their next meeting; and the said board shall order the compensation aforesaid to be paid out of the county treasury.

SEC. 70. It shall be the duty of the secretary of State to make out a complete form of poll books, tally lists, and all the forms required by this act, to be used by judges of election and the county clerks, and to send printed copies thereof to the county clerk of each county, and he shall cause to be printed in pamphlet form such parts of this act as are necessary for the guidance of the judges of election in the discharge of their duties, and to send printed copies thereof to the county clerk of each county, for him to distribute to the judges in each precinct or ward.

SEC. 71. No saloon or other place at which intoxicating liquors are sold shall be open during the day of any general or special election in this State. Any saloon-keeper or other person who shall sell, barter or give away any intoxicating liquors during the day of any general or special election, before the polls are closed on such day, shall for each and every offense, be liable to pay a fine of fifty dollars, or be imprisoned twenty days, or both, at the discretion of the court in which the case may be tried.

SEC. 72. The proper ballots, when not required to be taken from the ballot box for the purpose of election contests, shall remain in the ballot box in the custody of the county clerk and recorder until the next election, when, before opening the polls, the ballot box shall be opened in the presence of the judges, and the ballots destroyed by fire; *Provided*, That if the ballot boxes be needed for a special election before the legal time for commencing any proceedings in the way of contests shall have elapsed, or in case such judges at the time of holding of such special election, have knowledge of the pendency of any contest in which the ballots would be needed, the said judges shall preserve the ballots in some secure manner, and provide for their being so kept that no one can ascertain how any elector may have voted.

SEC. 73. Any person who shall falsely personate any voter, and vote under the name of such voter, shall, upon conviction, be punished by confinement and hard labor in the State penitentiary not exceeding three years.

SEC. 74. If any elector, challenged as unqualified, shall be guilty of wilful and corrupt false swearing or affirmation by any oath or affirmation prescribed by this act, such person shall be adjudged guilty of wilful and corrupt perjury.

SEC. 75. Every person who shall wilfully and corruptly procure any person to swear or affirm falsely as aforesaid shall be adjudged guilty of subornation of perjury, and shall, upon conviction thereof, suffer the punishment provided by law in cases of wilful and corrupt perjury.

SEC. 76. If any officer on whom any duty is enjoined by this act shall be guilty of any wilful neglect of such duty, or of any corrupt conduct in the execution of the same, and be thereof convicted, he shall be deemed guilty of a misdemeanor, punishable by fine or imprisonment, the fine in no case to exceed the sum of five hundred dollars, nor the imprisonment the term of one year.

SEC. 77. In case any judge of election shall knowingly and wilfully permit any person to vote at any election who is not entitled to vote thereat, the said judge so offending shall, on conviction thereof, be adjudged guilty of a misdemeanor, and shall be sentenced to pay a fine not exceeding five hundred dollars or be imprisoned in the county jail not exceeding six months.

SEC. 78. If any person shall, by bribery, menace, or other corrupt means or device whatsoever, either directly or indirectly, attempt to influence any voter of this State, in giving his vote or ballot, or deter him from giving the same, or disturb or hinder him in the free exercise of the right of suffrage at any election in this State, or shall fraudulently or deceitfully change or alter a ballot or cause any other deceit to be practiced with intent fraudulently to induce such elector to deposit the same as his vote, and thereby have the same thrown out and not counted, every person so offending against the provisions of this act shall be deemed guilty of a misdemeanor, punishable by fine not exceeding two hundred and fifty dollars or by imprisonment not exceeding six months.

SEC. 79. Any person who, at any general or special election, or any city or charter election, shall knowingly vote or offer to vote in any election precinct or ward in which he does not reside, shall, on conviction, be adjudged guilty of a misdemeanor, and punishable by fine not exceeding two hundred dollars, or by imprisonment not exceeding six months.

SEC. 80. If any elector shall accept or receive from any person whomsoever any money or other valuable thing for and in consideration of his voting for or against any person or persons who are candidates at any election in this State, he shall be deemed guilty of a misdemeanor, and punishable by a fine not exceeding two hundred dollars, or by imprisonment not exceeding six months.

SEC. 81. If any person shall mutilate or erase any name, figure or word in a poll book, taken or kept at any election; or if any person shall take away such poll book from the place where it has been deposited for safe keeping with an intention to destroy the same, or to procure or prevent the election of any person; or if any person shall destroy any poll book so taken and kept at any election, he or she shall be deemed guilty of a misdemeanor, and on conviction shall be fined not exceeding five hundred dollars or imprisoned not exceeding sixty days in the county jail.

SEC. 82. Any qualified elector may institute proceedings to contest the election of any person to the office of supreme, district or county judge. The supreme court shall have original jurisdiction for the adjudication of such contests, and shall prescribe rules for practice and proceedings therein.

Sec. 83. Any candidate or elector being desirous of contesting the election of any person declared elected governor, lieutenant-governor, secretary of State, auditor of State, treasurer of State, attorney-general, superintendent of public instruction, or regent of the university, shall, between the sixth and tenth days of the first session of the general assembly, after the day of election, file a notice of such intention with the secretary of the senate, specifying the particular points on which he means to rely.

Sec. 84. Upon any such notice being filed, as aforesaid, the general assembly shall, by resolution, determine on what day they will meet in joint convention to take action in any such contest, and thereupon a certified copy of the notice, filed by any contestor, shall be served upon the person whose election is sought to be contested, or by leaving a copy thereof at his last or usual place of residence, by such person as shall, by resolution, be appointed, with a notice that he is required to attend the joint convention, on the day so fixed, to answer the contest.

Sec. 85. On the hearing of any contested election for any of the offices named in section eighty-three of this act, the parties to such contest may introduce written testimony to be taken in manner later prescribed by the joint convention; but no depositions shall be read on such hearing unless the opposite party shall have had reasonable notice of the time and place of taking the same.

Sec. 86. In conducting any contested election for offices named in section eighty-three of this act, the following rules shall be observed, to-wit:

First—On the day and at the hour appointed for that purpose, the general assembly, with its proper officers, shall convene in joint convention.

Second—The president of the senate shall preside, but when he is the contestee, the president *pro tem.* of the senate shall preside.

Third—The parties to the contest shall then be called by the secretary of the senate, and if they answer, their appearance shall be recorded.

Fourth—The contestor shall first introduce his testimony, and then the contestee shall introduce his, and after the testimony is gone through on both sides, the contestor may, by himself or by his counsel, open the argument, and the contestee may then proceed, by himself or his counsel, to make his defense, and the contestor be heard in reply.

Fifth—After the arguments are thus gone through by the parties, any member of the joint convention shall be at liberty to offer his reasons for the vote he intends to give; *Provided,* That the convention may limit the time of argument and debate.

Sixth—The secretary of the senate shall keep a regular journal of the proceedings. The manner of taking the decision shall be by a call of the members, and a majority of all the votes given shall decide.

SEC. 87. The election of any person declared duly elected as a senator or member of the house of representatives, may be contested by any qualified voter of the county or district to be represented by such senator or representative.

SEC. 88. The contestor shall, within ten days after the canvass of the vote, serve on the contestee a statement, as hereinafter required, in relation to county officers, except the list of illegal votes, with a notice of taking depositions, if any are to be taken to be used at the trial.

SEC. 89. Any county judge or justice of the peace of a county in the district where the contest arises may issue subpœnas in the above cases, and shall have power to compel the attendance of witnesses, and depositions may be taken under the rules for taking depositions in the district courts.

SEC. 90. Copy of the statement and of the notices for taking depositions, with the service endorsed and verified by affidavit, if not served by an officer, shall be returned to the officer taking the deposition, and with the depositions shall be sealed up and transmitted by mail or by the hands of a sworn officer to the secretary of State, with an endorsement thereon, showing the nature of the papers, the names of the contesting parties, and the branch of the general assembly before which the contest is to be tried.

SEC. 91. The Secretary of State shall deliver the same, unopened, to the presiding officer of the house in which the contest is to be tried, on or before the fifth day of the session of the general assembly, and the presiding officer shall immediately give notice that such papers are in his possession.

SEC. 92. Nothing herein contained shall be construed to abridge the right of either branch of the general assembly to extend the time to take depositions, or to send for and examine any witness it may desire to hear on such trial.

SEC. 93. The election of any person declared duly elected to any county office, except the office of county judge, may be contested by any elector of the county.

First—For mal-conduct, fraud or corruption on the part of the judges of election in any precinct or ward, or any of the boards of canvassers, or on the part of any member of these boards.

Second—When the contestee is not eligible to the office to which he has been declared elected.

Third—When illegal votes have been received, or legal votes rejected at the polls, sufficient to change the result.

Fourth—For any error or mistake in any of the boards of judges or canvassers, in counting or in declaring the result of the election, if the error or mistake would affect the result.

Fifth—For any other cause (though not enumerated above) which shows that another was the legally elected person.

SEC. 94. The matter contained in the first, third and fourth causes of contest shall not be held sufficient to set aside the election, unless such causes be found sufficient to change the result.

SEC. 95. The judges before whom contested elections of county officers, except county judges, shall be tried and determined, shall be the county judge of the county in which the contest arises, and two disinterested justices of the peace of the same county; said justices to belong to different political parties when practicable, and to be selected by the county judge. Said judges shall sit together at the trial, and a judgment in which any two of them agree shall be a judgment in the case.

SEC. 96. The county clerk shall act as clerk at trials before said judges, and the proceedings therein shall be recorded in the records of the county court, the same as in any case in said county court, and if the county clerk is a party to any trial the said judges in such case shall appoint another person to act as their clerk. The contestor shall file in the office of the county clerk, within twenty days after the day when the votes are canvassed, a written statement of his intention to contest the election, setting forth the name of the contestor, and that he is an elector of the county; the name of the contestee; the office contested; the time of the election; and the particular causes of contest; which statement shall be verified by the affidavit of the contestor or some elector of the county, that the causes set forth are true as he verily believes. But before the county judge is required to take jurisdiction on the contest, the contestor must file with the judge or attorney a bond with security to be approved by said judge or attorney, and conditioned to pay all costs in case the election is confirmed, or the statement be dismissed, or the prosecution fails.

SEC. 97. When the reception of illegal or the rejection of legal votes is alleged as a cause of the contest, the number of persons who so voted or whose votes were rejected, and the precinct or ward where they voted or offered to vote shall be set forth in the statement.

SEC. 98. The county judge shall fix a day for the trial to commence not more than thirty nor less than twenty days after the notice of contest is filed, and shall thereupon forthwith issue notice to the contestee, which shall contain the time and place of trial, the name of contestant, and a brief statement of the causes of contest, which notice shall be served upon the contestee, by copy, by the sheriff of the county, at least fifteen days before the day of trial. The testimony may be oral, or by depositions taken before any justice of the peace or other officer authorized to take depositions, upon four days' notice.

Sec. 99. The style and form of process, the officers by whom served, and the manner of service of process and papers, and the fees of officers and witnesses, shall be the same as in the county court, so far as the nature of the case admits. The command to a witness may be to appear at ——— on ———, to testify in relation to a contested election wherein A—— B——— is contestor and C—— D——— contestee.

Sec. 100. The trial of contested elections shall take place at the county seat, unless adjourned to some other place within the county, by the concurrence of the court and the parties; and this court shall have all the powers incident to a court of record which may be necessary to the right hearing, conduct and determination of the matter before it.

Sec. 101. The court may direct the attendance of the sheriff or a constable when necessary.

Sec. 102. It shall be lawful to require any person called as a witness, who voted at such election, to an answer touching his qualifications as a voter; and if he was not a qualified voter in the precinct or ward in which he voted, and if the witness answers such questions, no part of his testimony shall be used against him in any criminal action, except for perjury in giving such testimony.

Sec. 103. If upon the trial of any contested election, for any officer mentioned in this act, it be proven that a vote or votes that were illegal were cast in any precinct or ward, the general assembly, senate, house of representatives, or the trial judges provided for in this act (as the case may be), shall have power, if such illegal vote or votes be sufficient to change the result, to send to the precinct or ward where such illegal voting was done, and obtain of their custodians the poll book and ballot box used at such election, and when so obtained, shall have the power to take out of the ballot box the ballots bearing the number corresponding to the number opposite the name on the poll book of the persons who have thus been proven to have voted illegally. The ballot or ballots so taken from the ballot box shall be examined, and if it be found that any or all of them bear the name of the contestee, they shall, or so many of them as do bear his name, be deducted from his vote, and the determination shall be in accordance with the result after such deduction shall have been made; *Provided,* That if it be found that illegal votes were cast for another person, they shall be deducted from such person's vote.

SEC. 104. The court shall pronounce judgment whether the contestee or any other person was duly elected, and the person so declared elected will be entitled to the office upon qualification. If the judgment be against the contestee, and he has received his certificate, the judgment annuls it. If the court finds that no person was duly elected, the judgment shall be that the election be set aside.

SEC. 105. The said judges shall be entitled to receive five dollars each per day for the time occupied by the trial, to be paid out of the county treasury.

SEC. 106. The contestor shall be liable to the officers and witnesses for all the costs made in the case, but if the judgment be against the contestee, or the election be set aside, the contestor shall have judgment in the amount of the costs against the contestee, to be recovered in like manner as upon executions issued out of the county court.

SEC. 107. Execution for costs shall be issued from the county court in election contest cases, in the same manner and with like effect as in any case pending or determined in the county court.

SEC. 108. After final judgment in any contested election case, the county judge shall have the same authority to enforce any order made at such trial, and the judgment therein, as in any case tried in the county court.

SEC. 109. Contested election of town and precinct officers shall be tried before the county board of canvassers in the same manner as is provided by law for contesting elections of county officers, so far as the same is practicable.

SEC. 110. The judges of elections in the several wards and election precincts shall meet on Tuesday, three weeks before the day upon which any general election shall by law be appointed to be held, at nine o'clock a. m. of said day, and proceed to make a registry list, as hereinafter prescribed, of the names of all persons qualified and entitled to vote at the ensuing election in the ward or precinct in which they are judges, which list, when completed and revised as hereinafter provided, shall constitute the registry of electors of said precinct. Whenever at the last election in any precinct, prior to the meeting of such board of registry, the number of votes cast in such precinct shall have exceeded three hundred, the said board may continue in session for the purpose of making such registry, five days if necessary; when the number of votes cast in such precinct shall have exceeded one hundred, the said board may continue in session, for the purpose of making such registry, three days if necessary, otherwise but one day.

SEC. 111. The list so made shall contain the names of the qualified electors of the ward or voting precinct in which the same is made, alphabetically arranged, according to surnames, so as to show in one column the names of each elector at full length, and in another the place of his residence, designated by the number or name of street, and number of house, if known, or the section or other subdivision thereof, according to United States surveys, on which such elector shall reside, if he reside on surveyed lands, and if not, such description as will best locate his residence. Said board shall enter on said list the names of all legally qualified electors in such ward or precinct, or of those who will become such by lapse of time, on or before the next ensuing day of such general election, as aforesaid, in all cases in which such entry can be made consistent with the provisions hereinafter contained. For the convenience of the said board they are authorized to take from the office of the county clerk the poll list of such ward or precinct, filed by the judges of the last preceding election in such precinct. Said board shall make four copies of such registry list when revised and completed, which list they shall certify to be correct, and forward one copy to the office of the county clerk, and retain two copies for use on election day; and one copy they shall, within two days from the completion thereof, post in some conspicuous place where the last election was held in such precinct, and so as to be accessible and convenient to any elector who may desire to inspect the same. The board of county commissioners may cause to be printed and published any such registry list when completed, at an expense not exceeding two cents per name thereon.

SEC. 112. Every board of registry shall meet on the Tuesday of the week preceding any and every general election, at the place designated for holding such election, for the purpose of revising, correcting and completing such registry list, and in all cases they shall meet at nine o'clock a. m. and remain in session until six o'clock of said day. Said boards of registry shall meet at the place designated for holding such election, on the day preceding the election, at nine o'clock a. m., and remain in session until six o'clock p. m. of the same day, at which time any elector whose name is not on the revised registry list may have his name placed thereon; *Provided*, He shall take and subscribe to the oath prescribed in section forty of this act, and shall prove by the oath of two registered electors of the precinct (or ward) that such person has been a resident of the precinct ten days, of the county thirty days, and of the State six months next preceding the day of election, and that they verily believe him to be a qualified elector. Said oaths shall be taken and subscribed to in the presence of the board of registry, either of whom may administer the oath; and said oaths shall be preserved and filed in the office of the county clerk, together with the poll lists of said election. The name of such person and his residence, as given by him, shall be entered upon the registry list, and opposite the name of such person shall be marked the word "affidavit" and the names of the witnesses.

SEC. 113. No vote shall be received at any election unless the name of the person offering to vote shall be found on the said certified registry list.

SEC. 114. In cases of vacancy in the office of judge of election, or in the board of registry, at any time when they meet according to law, the vacancy may be filled by the election, by the qualified electors then present, of a

5e

qualified elector to serve as a member of such board of registry until the appearance of a judge of election duly appointed in and for such ward or precinct.

Sec. 115. Every judge of elections or other person serving on such board of registry shall, before entering upon the duties of his office, take an oath, to be administered by any justice of the peace or other officer present having power to administer oaths, faithfully to discharge the duties of registrar according to law and to the best of his skill and ability. If no such officer shall be present the oath may be administered by one judge or registrar to another.

Sec. 116. The members of said board of registry shall receive the same compensation as allowed by law to judges of elections, for every day actually employed in the making and completing of the registry.

Sec. 117. It shall be the duty of the secretary of State to make out a complete form of a registry book, alphabetically arranged, with the oath of the registrar in blank, and the requisite blank columns properly headed, and have the same printed, and to send copies thereof to the county clerk of each county in the State, together with a sufficient number of copies of the registry and election laws bound in pamphlet form

Sec. 118. It shall be the duty of the county clerk of each county to furnish annually for the use of the board of registry in each precinct or ward in his county, four printed copies of said blank registries, and send them by mail or other safe conveyance to the judges of elections in such wards or precincts at least twenty (20) days prior to the day of the first meeting of the board of registry as herein provided.

Sec. 119. The persons appointed judges of election in every incorporated town or city, hereafter, shall meet on Tuesday of the week preceding each municipal election in [the] town or city in which they are such judges, in the several precincts, at the place of holding municipal elections therein, for the purpose of revising, correcting and completing the annual registry in this act required to be made, and for that purpose they are authorized to take from the office of the county clerk the last annual registry of electors of the wards or precincts, including the town or city in which they are appointed judges.

SEC. 120. The last mentioned registrars shall, in all respects, proceed in the revising and correcting of their respective wards or precincts as is hereinbefore provided for in the revision and correcting of the annual registries, except that the registry list, as so revised and corrected by such city or town registrars, shall be filed with the city or town clerk of the proper city or town.

SEC. 121. All registries taken from the county clerk's office under the provisions of the last section, shall be returned to the county clerk within ten (10) days after the day of registry for which they may be taken out of the same.

SEC. 122. The same proceedings shall be had in all cases of special elections as are herein provided for general elections, so far as the same may be applicable.

SEC. 123. All judges of election shall, on being appointed, hold their office for one (1) year, or until their successors are appointed, and shall serve at all special elections during their term of office, and they shall severally before entering upon their duties as judges at any election take and subscribe the oath prescribed by law in such cases.

SEC. 124. In case any new election precinct shall be formed, the county commissioners shall immediately appoint judges of election therein: and in the case of the division of any voting precinct, the names of all voters residing in that part of any precinct stricken off shall be stricken from the registry list in the voting precinct from which such part shall have been stricken, and shall be inserted in the registry lists of the precinct to which such part may have been attached, at the first registration of voters' names in each such precinct respectively.

SEC. 125. That hereafter the judges of elections, when acting as a board of registry in cases provided by law, shall not, in any case, allow the name of any person to be placed on the list of registered voters, called the registry of elections, in any ward or voting precinct in this State, unless in the following cases:

First—When the person whose name is to be registered, and also the facts of his legal qualification as a voter in the ward, township or precinct in which such registry is made, shall be known to one or more of the persons acting as such board of registry, and the judge or person so acting on such board of registry to whom such voter and his legal qualifications are known shall sign his name on the registry roll or list opposite the name of such voter, and the judge or person acting as member of such board of registry so signing his name opposite the name of such voter, shall be deemed and held to have vouched under oath that such person so registered is a legal voter within the ward, township or precinct in which such registry is made; and such judge or person acting on such board of registry who shall sign his own name as aforesaid shall be subject to the same liability in all respects as a person making affidavit under the provisions of the next following clause of this section.

Secondly—When a legal voter being registered in such ward, township or precinct, and known as such by one or more of such judges or person acting on such board of registry, or proven to be such by affidavit of some known legal voter, registered in such ward, township or precinct, in similar form to that herein following, shall make affidavit in substance as follows:

I, ———, do solemnly swear, in the presence of the ever-living God, that I am a resident and a legal voter in ——— ward (precinct), in the county of ———, State of Colorado, and that I well know ——— ———, who aims to be registered as a legal voter in said ——— ward (precinct), and I know that he has resided in the State of Colorado during six months, in ——— county thirty days last past, and has resided in said ward during ten days last past, and still resides therein, and his place of residence is at No. ——— ——— street, (on ——— of section No. ——,) in said ward ——— (precinct), and I believe him to be of lawful age.

The blanks therein filled with the proper names, dates, places and numbers, as the case may require, and such affidavit shall show that the person so offering to vote is or will be by the day of election next ensuing in all respects a legal voter in such ward or precinct.

SEC. 126. Every judge of election, or person acting as such on any board of registry, who shall wilfully set his name on the registry roll opposite the name of any voter registered on such list, knowing him to be not legally entitled to be registered upon such list, shall be deemed guilty of a misdemeanor, and upon conviction thereof shall be punished by fine of not less than three hundred (300) dollars nor more than one thousand (1,000) dollars; or be imprisoned not less than thirty (30) days nor more than ninety (90) days, or may be punished by both such fine and imprisonment.

SEC. 127. If any person shall make an affidavit, as provided in section one hundred and twenty-six of this act, for the purpose of causing the name of any person to be registered in any ward or precinct in this State, and shall in such affidavit state falsely the name of such person to be registered, or the fact of his having resided in such precinct or ward a sufficient length of time to entitle him to be so registered, or the place of his actual habitation or residence, or the fact of his age or of his residence within a sufficient time to entitle him to be registered, the person so making a false affidavit shall be deemed guilty of a wilful and corrupt perjury, and on conviction shall be punished accordingly.

SEC. 128. Every person who shall procure his own name or the name of any other person to be registered on the list of registered voters called the registry list, in any ward or voting precinct in this State in which any election is or may be by law authorized to be held, and in which ward or precinct such person shall not be at the time of such registry entitled to be registered in such ward or voting precinct; or if any person shall procure or attempt to procure to be registered in any ward or voting precinct any fictitious name as the name of any person entitled to be registered in such ward or precinct, every person so procuring or attempting to procure such registry of the name of any person not by law entitled to be registered, or any fictitious name in manner aforesaid, shall be deemed guilty of a misdemeanor, and upon conviction thereof shall be fined not less than two hundred (200) dollars, nor more than five hundred (500) dollars, or be imprisoned not less than ten (10) nor more than forty (40) days for each and every offense, or may be punished by both such fine and imprisonment.

SEC. 129. The registry of voters' names shall be completed on the evening next preceding each and every election appointed by law to be held in each and every precinct, and no names shall be added to the registry list in any ward or precinct after the close of the registration on the day preceding such election; and in case any judge of election or person acting as member of any board of registry shall wilfully and knowingly add any name or names of any person, or any fictitious or false name to the list of registered voters in any ward or voting precinct after the close of the registry of voters' names, on the next day preceding any election in such ward or voting precinct according to law, shall be deemed guilty of a misdemeanor, and on conviction thereof shall be punished by a fine of not less than two hundred (200) dollars, nor more than five hundred (500) dollars for each and every offense.

SEC. 130. All fines or forfeitures collected under the provisions of this act shall be paid to the county treasurer of the county wherein the offense was committed for the benefit of the school fund of such county.

SEC. 131. That all acts and parts of acts enacted by any territorial legislature relating to elections be and the same are hereby repealed.

SEC. 132. All ballots shall be written on plain white paper, or printed with black ink with a space of not less than one-fifth of an inch between each name, on plain white news printing paper, not more than two and one-half inches nor less than two and three-eighths inches wide, without any device or mark by which one ticket may be known or distinguished from another, except the words at the head of the tickets; and it shall be unlawful for any person to print for distribution at the polls, or distribute to any elector or voter, any ballot printed or written contrary to the provisions hereof, but this section shall not be considered to prohibit the erasure, correction or insertion of any name by pencil or with ink upon the face of the printed ballot.

SEC. 133. When a ballot with a certain designated heading contains printed thereon in place of another a name not found on the regular ballot having such heading, such name shall be regarded by the judges as having been placed thereon for the purpose of fraud, and such ballot shall not be counted for the name so found. .

SEC. 134. If a ballot contains a greater number of names for any one office than the number of persons required to fill that office, it shall be considered fraudulent as to all of the names designated to fill such office, but no further. A ballot shall not be considered fraudulent if containing a less number of names than are authorized to be inserted.

SEC. 135. That whenever an election shall be ordered by the board of county commissioners of any county to ascertain the sense of the legal voters of such county upon the question of removal or location of the county seat of such county, it shall be the duty of such board of county commissioners to appoint special judges and registers of such elections, and to provide s special ballot box in each voting precinct, in which shall be deposited all the ballots cast at such election in such precinct on the question of location or removal of the county seat.

SEC. 136. It shall be the duty of the judges and registers so appointed to make a special registration of the voters of each precinct who have resided in the county at least six months and in such precinct at least ninety days prior to the day designated for holding such election, which day shall be the day designated by law for holding a general election, and no other.

SEC. 137. The election shall be held at the same places at which the general election is ordered to be held, but the vote for or against removal for location of the county seat shall be by a special ballot, separate and distinct from the general ticket voted at said election, which ballot shall be deposited in the special ballot box provided for in section 1st [one] of this act, and no vote shall be counted for or against said removal or location which is not deposited in such special ballot box as herein provided.

Sec. 138. No county seat shall be removed until the expiration of thirty days after the canvass of the votes had by the county canvassers upon the question of location or removal, nor until the board of county commissioners of such county shall have made and entered of record on their journal an order directing such removal, which order the said board shall make within thirty (30) days after the county canvass is completed, unless enjoined or restrained from so doing by an order of the district court of said county or the judge thereof, or by the supreme court.

Sec. 139. All laws now in force relating to elections shall apply to elections held upon the question of removal or location of county seats, except that the question of location of such county seat shall be contested in the district court of said county in the first instance, but may be removed to the district court of any other county under the provisions of the code relating to change of the place of trial, and shall be also subject to appeal or writ of error to the supreme court; *Provided*, That not less than two-thirds of all the legal votes cast shall be necessary to effect the removal of the county seat of any county in this State.

Sec. 140. All laws governing contests of elections shall be held applicable to contests of county seat elections except that the board of county commissioners of the county shall in all cases be the contestee, and that the contest shall be conducted in the district court of the proper county. Such district court, or the judge thereof in vacation, may appoint a referee to take testimony in relation to the grounds of contest alleged by the contestor, which referee may sit to take evidence in any precinct of his county.

Sec. 141. Any committee or body authorized by the rules or customs of a voluntary political association or organization to call primary elections of or for such association or organization, for any purpose, may, by resolution adopted at the time of making the call, elect to have such elections conducted in accordance with the provisions of this act.

Sec. 142. The resolution must declare:

First—The time and place of holding the election and the hours between which the polls are to be kept open; *Provided, however,* That in precincts having more than one hundred (100) voters the polls shall be opened not less than five hours before sunset and continue open not less than six hours; in precincts having less than one hundred (100) voters the polls shall be opened three hours before sunset, and be kept open not less than two hours.

Second—The object of the election.

Third—The names of three persons to act as judges of the election at each precinct.

Fourth—That such election will be held under the provisions of the primary election law.

Fifth—The time and manner of the publication of notice of such election.

Sixth—The qualifications required for voters in addition to those prescribed by law.

Sec. 143. The notice of the election must be signed by the secretary of the committee or body, and must contain a copy of the resolution and be published as directed in the resolution; but not less than one week's notice shall be given.

Sec. 144. The qualifications of voters at any primary election held under this act shall be:

First—Such qualifications as are prescribed by an act entitled "an act to amend section 1, of chapter 30, of the general laws of Colorado, in relation to elections, and repealing all laws inconsistent with this act," approved February 18th, 1881.

Second—Such additional qualifications as are required by the resolution referred to in the previous sections of this act; *Provided, however,* That in all cases where a person offering to vote is challenged, he shall swear that he is a member *bona fide* of the party holding such primary election before his vote shall be received.

Sec. 145. All primary elections held under this act shall be held and conducted in accordance with the rules and under the penalties prescribed by chapter thirty of the general laws of the State of Colorado, from and including section twenty-five of said chapter to section fifty-two thereof inclusive, except sections thirty-one, thirty-six and fifty-one.

Sec. 146. The judge to whom any ticket may be delivered shall upon the receipt thereof pronounce in an audible voice the name of the voter, and if no objection be made to him, and the judges are satisfied that he is a legal and qualified voter at such primary election, the ballot shall be numbered and immediately be put in the ballot box without inspecting the name or names written or printed thereon. And the clerks of election shall enter the name of the voter and number in the poll books.

Sec. 147. In addition to the challenges allowed by section thirty-eight of chapter thirty of the general laws any person offering to vote at a primary election held under this act may be challenged upon the grounds that he does not possess the other qualifications prescribed by the resolution of the committee or body referred to in sections one and two of this act, and such challenge must be tried and determined by the judges, who, to that end, may administer an oath or affirmation to such person, and may ask him any question tending to prove or disprove the challenge.

Sec. 148. None but persons who possess the qualifications prescribed by the provisions of the said act, approved February 18, 1881, and by the resolution referred to in the previous sections of this act, shall vote or participate in any of the proceedings at such primary elections. Any person not possessing such qualifications, who shall vote or participate in any of the proceedings at such election, shall be guilty of a misdemeanor, and on conviction thereof before a justice of the peace of the county in which such offense was committed shall be punished by a fine not less than fifty (50) dollars nor exceeding three hundred (300) dollars, or by imprisonment not less than one month nor exceeding three months, or by both such fine and imprisonment.

SEC. 149. As soon as all the votes cast at an election held under this act shall have been read off and counted, the judges of election shall make out a certificate under their hands and attested by the clerks, stating the number of votes each candidate received, and designating the office or position for which such person received such vote or votes, the number being expressed in words at full length and in numerical figures. The said certificate, together with the ballots cast, and one of the lists of voters and one of the tally lists, which shall be signed and attested in like manner as the certificate, shall be enclosed and sealed up under cover and delivered to the secretary signing the notice of election, or in the event of the death or absence from the county of such secretary, then to any member of the committee or body calling said primary election.

SEC. 150. The judges of the primary election must keep a copy of said certificate and one of the lists of voters for twenty days after the election.

SEC. 151. The committee or body from which emanated the resolution calling the election shall, under such rules as it may adopt, open and canvass the returns, and issue certificates to persons chosen to fill offices or positions by the voters at such election, designating the offices or positions to which they have been elected or chosen.

SEC. 152. If any person shall, by bribery, menace, threatening or other corrupt means or device whatsoever, either directly or indirectly, attempt to influence any voter in giving his vote at any primary election held under this act, every person so offending shall, on conviction, be fined not less than one hundred (100) dollars nor exceeding five hundred (500) dollars, and shall be imprisoned not less than three months nor exceeding twelve months in the county jail.

SEC. 153. If any person offering to vote, and being challenged as disqualified, shall be guilty of wilful and corrupt false swearing or affirmation by any oath or affirmation prescribed by this act, or by the provisions of the sections of chapter thirty of the general laws hereinbefore referred to, or shall suborn any other person to swear or affirm as aforesaid, such person shall be deemed guilty of perjury or subornation of perjury, as the case may be, and upon conviction thereof shall be punished by confinement in the penitentiary for a term not less than one year nor more than fourteen years.

SEC. 154. If any judge or clerk of a primary election held under this act, or any other officer upon whom a duty is enjoined by this act, shall be guilty of any wilful neglect of such duty, or of any corrupt conduct in the execution of the same, and be thereof convicted, he shall be deemed guilty of a misdemeanor, and punished by a fine not less than one hnndred (100) dollars, nor exceeding five hundred (500) dollars, or by imprisonment not less than three months nor exceeding one year in the county jail, or by both such fine and imprisonment

www.ingramcontent.com/pod-product-compliance
Lightning Source LLC
Chambersburg PA
CBHW032135080426
42733CB00008B/1089